FESTIVALS OF THE WORLD
FRANCE

W
FRANKLIN WATTS
LONDON • SYDNEY

This edition first published in 2006 by
Franklin Watts
338 Euston Road
London
NW1 3BH

This edition is published for sale only in the United
Kingdom & Eire.

© Marshall Cavendish International (Asia) Pte Ltd 2006
Originated and designed by Marshall Cavendish
International (Asia) Pte Ltd
A member of Times Publishing Limited
Times Centre, 1 New Industrial Road
Singapore 536196

Written by: Susan McKay
Edited by: Katharine Brown-Carpenter
Designed by: Sri Putri Julio
Picture research: Thomas Khoo and Joshua Ang

A CIP catalogue record for this book is available from the
British Library.

ISBN 0 7496 6770 2

Dewey Classification: 394.26944

Printed in Malaysia

CONTENTS

It's Festival Time . . .

The French are noted throughout the world for two things – their style and their food. Festival time in France is no different. Here you can taste delicious foods, sip first-class wines and enjoy the wonders of a French *fête*. Fancy some Celtic dancing, a magnificent float parade or a day with the Gypsies? Well, come along and join in the fun. It's fête time in France …

WHERE'S FRANCE?

France is one of the oldest nations in Europe. It lies near the edge of the continent and has a long coastline on the Atlantic Ocean. There are many different landforms in France – mountains, forests, plains, beaches and volcanoes. The capital, and the largest city, is Paris.

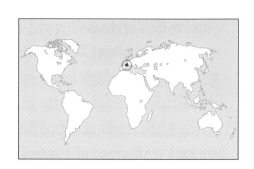

A French girl holding two **baguettes**, the delicious, crusty bread made famous by the French.

Who are the French?

Thousands of years ago, France was invaded by a tribe of people known as the **Celts**. The Celts had a love of art and a great respect for nature. Many Celtic traditions are reflected in the customs and practices of the French, especially in the region of Brittany on the north-west coast.

Many years later, people from all over Europe travelled across the continent. When they reached France, they thought they had reached the edge of the world (the Americas had not been discovered yet). These people settled in France and made it their home.

Today, the French people are a mix of many different ethnic backgrounds.

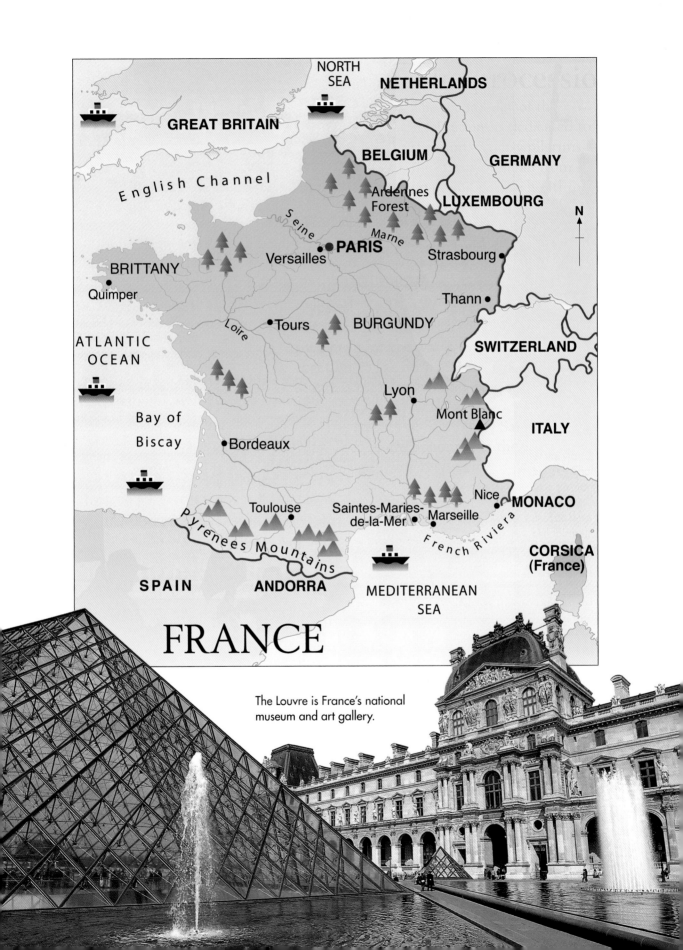

NORTH
SEA

NETHERLANDS

GREAT BRITAIN

BELGIUM

GERMANY

English Channel

Ardennes
Forest

LUXEMBOURG

Seine

Marne

PARIS

Strasbourg

Versailles

BRITTANY

Quimper

Thann

Loire

Tours

BURGUNDY

SWITZERLAND

ATLANTIC
OCEAN

Lyon

Mont Blanc

ITALY

Bay of
Biscay

Bordeaux

Nice

MONACO

Toulouse

Saintes-Maries-
de-la-Mer

Marseille

Pyrenees Mountains

French Riviera

CORSICA
(France)

SPAIN

ANDORRA

MEDITERRANEAN
SEA

N

FRANCE

The Louvre is France's national
museum and art gallery.

WHEN'S THE FÊTE?

SPRING
- ✪ **MAY DAY** ✪ **THE GYPSY FESTIVAL**
- ✪ **ST. JOAN OF ARC DAY** – Remembers the great warrior who fought for the French cause.
- ✪ **ST. BERNARD OF MONTJOUX** – Honours the patron saint of mountain climbers who made the Alpine passes safe for travellers.

Don't we look smart in our special outfits? Turn to page 8 to see more at the Cornouaille Festival.

SUMMER
- ✪ **SAILOR'S DAY** – Boats are decorated with thousands of paper flowers and blessed by a priest. Children parade through the streets to the church with handmade models of ships on platforms.
- ✪ **BASTILLE DAY**
- ✪ **PROCESSION OF THE BOTTLES** – Men walk through the town of Boulbon carrying bottles of new wine. All the men uncork their bottles at the same time and swallow a mouthful of wine.
- ✪ **CORPUS CHRISTI** – Christians eat bread and wine. They believe that Jesus is present in them.
- ✪ **ST. JOHN'S DAY** – People light bonfires and set barrels on fire before rolling them down hills.
- ✪ **BURNING OF THE THREE FIRS** – People in Thann burn three fir trees in memory of the founding of the town.
- ✪ **TOUR DE FRANCE** – Teams of 10 cyclists race daily for three weeks to circle the country.
- ✪ **CORNOUAILLE FESTIVAL**

AUTUMN

- ✪ **DAY OF THE FLUTES** – Musicians parade through the streets playing ancient instruments.
- ✪ **ST. CRISPIN'S DAY** – People go to church to honour the patron saint of shoes.
- ✪ **LA QUINTANE** – Thirty men carry a box painted like a prison to the church where it is blessed. Later, they hit the box with mallets until it is smashed to bits.
- ✪ **GRAPE HARVEST FESTIVALS**
- ✪ **ST. CATHERINE'S DAY** – Unmarried women over 25 receive a special dinner and wear fancy hats at their parade.

Pick up your flag and march to the sea. It's time to party in Cannes!

WINTER

- ✪ **ST. NICHOLAS DAY** – St. Nicholas gives gifts to children who have been good throughout the year.
- ✪ **CHRISTMAS EVE** – French families gather for a traditional supper after midnight mass.
- ✪ **CHRISTMAS**
- ✪ **EPIPHANY** – Cakes are baked with coins inside them. Whoever gets the piece of cake with the coin is the king or queen for the day.
- ✪ **NEW YEAR'S DAY**
- ✪ **ST. BERNADETTE OF LOURDES**
- ✪ **CARNAVAL**

7

CORNOUAILLE FESTIVAL

For 70 years, the people of Brittany have been celebrating the Cornouaille Festival. Between the third and fourth Sundays in July, the town of Quimper (check the map on page 5) in the district of Cornouaille becomes the capital of Breton culture.

Blowing the trumpet to celebrate years of Breton culture.

A time to remember

Over the seven days of the festival, there are 200 shows, hundreds of musicians, thousands of dancers, puppet shows and traditional Breton games. Sound like fun? It sure is. But the people of Brittany have another good reason for holding the festival every year – to preserve their heritage and remember their roots. For young people, Bretons and non-Bretons alike, the Cornouaille Festival offers a chance to learn about Celtic music, history, food and dance. People come from far and wide to see the shows and to relive history. Keep reading and learn more about this fascinating culture.

This little girl is dressed and ready for the Cornouaille Festival. You can read more about her special clothes on page 10.

Where's Brittany?

Brittany is a region in north-western France. It is the home of tiny fishing villages and huge seaports. The people of Brittany are called Bretons. Many of them still speak an ancient language called Celtic, which was handed down by the original settlers of France, the Celts. There are some Bretons who think the best way to preserve their culture is to separate from the rest of France. What do you think?

Who were the Celts?

The Celts were a people who once lived throughout Europe. They settled in France about 2,500 years ago. They were bound by language, art and respect for nature. The Celts were also fierce warriors who drove chariots and fought battles.

You can see many similarities between Breton culture and that of other Celtic nations, such as Ireland, Scotland and Wales.

Bretons perform traditional Celtic dances as part of the festivities.

Breton dress

Brittany is famous for lacemaking, and Breton dress is an excellent way for lacemakers to show off their skills.

Breton women wear embroidered bodices and full skirts that reach to the floor. They also wear a **coiffe**, a special hat made of lace. The lace is attached to a base so that it stands straight up. The coiffe can measure up to 45 centimetres high! In the old days, you could tell which region a woman came from by the hat she wore. You could also tell if she was single or married by her clothes.

Men wear baggy trousers called **bragon bas**. They are worn to the knee and are usually made of cotton. Their vests or waistcoats are embroidered. The outfit is completed with a wide-brimmed hat and **sabots**, special clogs worn on their feet.

The parade

On the first Sunday of the Cornouaille Festival, the town organises a huge parade. Townspeople and visitors take part to show off their beautiful costumes. The parade is led by more than 500 musicians playing bagpipes, trumpets and drums. The procession winds through the cobbled streets of Quimper in a blur of black and white.

The procession through Quimper is a display of the beautiful costumes worn by Bretons.

Bagpipes were originally made from sheepskins and goatskins. Today, they are generally made of cloth.

Think about this

The legends of King Arthur and Merlin are some of the best-loved stories in France. Arthur's father, Uther Pendragon, was the king of Brittany. His mother, Ygerne, was the duchess of Cornouaille.

BASTILLE DAY

A special day in France is 14 July. Not only does it commemorate a very important date in French history, it is also France's national day. And that can only mean one thing – it's time to have a party! More than one million people stream into Paris during the month of July just to take part in the festivities. Come along and we'll show you how to party French style!

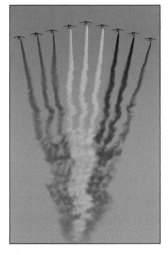

The air show is one of the highlights of the day.

Why is it called Bastille Day?

The Bastille was a castle built in the 14th century. It was later converted into a prison. On 14 July 1789, Parisians stormed the prison. They freed the prisoners and took the building apart stone by stone. For the French people, the Bastille was a symbol of their **oppression** by the king and queen. The storming of the Bastille marked the beginning of the French Revolution, a struggle that helped the people gain their independence. You can read more about the French Revolution on page 15.

A monument now stands in Paris on the site of the Bastille. On Bastille Day, it is decorated with French flags.

Opposite: Fireworks explode over the Arc de Triomphe.

12

Bastille Day celebrations

The festivities to honour Bastille Day start early in the morning. The daylight hours are reserved for military parades and brass bands. At night, buildings are brightly lit and firecrackers are set off in the street. At 10:30, the official fireworks display begins. Red, white and blue lights fill the sky in celebration of French nationalism. People cheer and wave their flags. The French flag is called *tricolore*, or three colours, because it is decorated with three bands of colour – red, white and blue.

People congregate at the monument to the Bastille, where they can listen to bands or join in the dancing that spills into the street. Each year, fire stations in Paris sponsor a huge dinner and ball. Firefighters dress in full uniform and wait on tables. They also play accordions to accompany the dancing.

Military parades mark the day when the French celebrate their nation.

The French Revolution

In the 18th century, the people of France were tired of the way King Louis XVI was running the country. The commoners were treated unfairly and, while the rich became richer, the poor could barely survive.

The storming of the Bastille was the beginning of a wave of changes that took place in France. A new constitution was written and the Declaration of the Rights of Man and of the Citizen declared that "Men are born and remain free and equal in rights". By working together, the French people had won a democratic government.

King Louis XVI (*above*) and his wife, Marie Antoinette, were both beheaded by the new government after their defeat in the **revolution**.

Napoleon Bonaparte

Napoleon Bonaparte was a young and brilliant soldier who became the hero of the French people during the revolution. In 1804, he crowned himself emperor. Led by Napoleon, the French forces took over large parts of Europe. They were defeated by the English at the Battle of Waterloo in Belgium in 1815. After the French defeat, the country was weak. The royal family tried to return to power but they were defeated by the French people in two more revolutions in 1830 and 1848.

Napoleon Bonaparte as emperor.

Think about this
The Arc de Triomphe, a famous monument in Paris, was built to celebrate the great military victories of Emperor Bonaparte. On the walls of the Arc is a list of his great victories. His defeats are not mentioned.

CARNAVAL

For 12 days in February, the southern city of Nice (find Nice on the map on page 5) falls under a spell. Is it witchcraft? No, it's the annual Carnaval festivities at their best. The rest of France celebrates Carnaval as well, but nowhere are the decorations more elaborate and the merrymaking more spirited than in Nice. Keep reading and we'll take you on a tour of this beautiful city which has been celebrating Carnaval since the 13th century – over 700 years!

These golden masks are a common sight all over France during Carnaval.

Mardi Gras

You may know the French term *Mardi Gras* from the famous Carnival that takes place in New Orleans every year. *Mardi Gras* means 'Fat Tuesday', which is another name for Shrove Tuesday. It is the day before Ash Wednesday, also the first day of Lent. Traditionally, Fat Tuesday was the day on which all eggs, fats and other foods forbidden during Lent were eaten. It was also the day people confessed their sins. The name Shrove Tuesday comes from the old word *shrive*, which means 'forgiveness'. Christians hope to be forgiven for all their sins on this day.

Huge groups of people dress in costumes with papier-mâché masks. They are known as the 'big heads'.

Ordinary costumes just won't do at the Nice Carnaval.

17

The Battle of Flowers

Flowers used to make perfume are grown in the south of France. Flowers have also been an important part of the Carnaval celebrations for a long time. During the 12 days of celebration, all the floats, and many of the costumes for the parade, are made from flowers and other plants.

One tradition that has become popular in Nice is battling with flowers. The first battle is between the floats. The crowd argues over which is the most beautiful. Later in the afternoon, the real battles begin. Everyone buys a huge bunch of flowers and, at the signal, they let them fly. No one is safe, so it's best to have a good supply of ammunition. When the fighting is finally over, everyone is covered in petals and stems.

Even the costumes are made from flowers!

Opposite: A lot of work goes into making the floats. This one of a pirate on his ship may have taken months to create.

Below: Brass bands accompany the parade and entertain the onlookers.

How did the battles begin?

Throwing flowers is an ancient tradition. Many years ago, flowers were thrown as part of a fertility rite. It is very similar to the tradition of throwing rice or confetti at a wedding to wish the bride and groom good luck in the future.

Think about this?
When French students went to study in New Orleans in the 1800s, they missed the Mardi Gras celebrations from home. They introduced Carnaval to their new country. The New Orleans celebrations were famous across the world.

THE GYPSY FESTIVAL

Each year in May, the small town of Saintes-Maries-de-la-Mer (Saint Marys of the Sea) is the site of one of the largest Gypsy gatherings in the world. The Gypsies travel from far and wide to the coast of France to honour their patron saint, Sarah. The festival celebrates Sarah's annual return to the shores of the Mediterranean Sea. For two days, the fiesta spirit takes over the town. The sound of Gypsy music can be heard from one end of the town to the other.

The legend of the saints

The legend of the saints who gave their names to the town dates back to Biblical times. Mary Salome and Mary Jacobe were the mothers of two **apostles**. They were forced to leave Palestine in a boat with no oars or sails. Sarah, a dark-skinned woman from Egypt, guided them to the shores of France, where they built an **oratory** and spread the word of Christ.

Among the Gypsies, Sarah is known as Sarah la Kali, or Sarah the Dark One.

The procession

The second day of the celebrations is dedicated to the saints. Gypsy pilgrims take the statue of Sarah from her **crypt** and parade her through the streets of the town in a procession. The statue is accompanied by the chorus of the crowd, crying "Long live Saint Sarah! Long live the Gypsies!" Eventually, the procession reaches its destination – the beach – and everyone makes a mad dash for the water. Gypsies and *gadje* come together to ask for a blessing from God. The statue is then loaded on a boat and taken out to sea for a final blessing.

The statues of Saint Mary Salome and Saint Mary Jacobe are honoured in the same way.

The two Marys are carried to the seaside on a litter. They are honoured as well but, for the Gypsies, it is Sarah's day.

The local townspeople take part in the procession as well.

The Gypsy capital

For the two days of this festival, this small southern town becomes the capital of the Gypsies. Over the years, the festival has drawn some of the most famous Gypsy entertainers in the world. When the music gets going, heels begin to click and hands to clap. Soon, everyone is singing and dancing in time with the music.

The festival is also a popular time for weddings and baptisms, which are postponed all year so they can be blessed properly by Saint Sarah.

A young Gypsy girl dressed up for the occasion.

Opposite: Bullfights and horse shows are one of the main attractions.

The locals take to the streets wearing traditional regional dress.

The Wild South

Once the Gypsies have finished their business, they are eager to get back on the road. But for those with time on their hands, the celebrations continue the next day with a rodeo. Saintes-Maries-de-la-Mer is in an area of France known as the Camargue. The Camargue is the Wild South of France, where cowboys and wild horses are a common sight. For the remainder of the week, the people of the Camargue put on their own show.

Think about this
Gypsies originally came from northern India, but now they can be found worldwide. They are known as travellers who move from one place to the next according to the seasons. In many countries, Gypsies are the guardians of tradition.

GRAPE HARVEST FESTIVALS

F rance is famous throughout the world for its wines. Every autumn, in the wine-producing areas of France, the local people celebrate the end of the grape harvest. The French call the harvest *la vendange*. They hold dances and taste the new wine for the first time. Members of wine societies dress in traditional robes to test the grapes and wines. Farmers and townspeople celebrate the end of the grape-growing season.

Robed men test the newly harvested grapes.

Most people in France drink wine. Even children are allowed to have a small glass on special occasions.

This wine is kept in oak barrels, which adds to its flavour and aroma.

A barrel of laughs

One of the biggest harvest festivals takes place in the region of Burgundy, where three great wine-producing areas host Les Trois Glorieuses. This refers to the three glorious days in November when French people from all over the country indulge in wine tasting and folk dancing. It is also the country's most important wine auction.

Citizens of Verdigny celebrate the Festival of the New Grapes with much pomp and ceremony. Wine tasters in proper ceremonial dress sip the wine slowly before making judgments on its flavour and quality.

Even long after the harvesting season is over, the French continue to celebrate by honouring the patron saint of wine, Saint Vincent. His day falls on 22 January. It is celebrated mostly by people in the villages.

THINGS FOR YOU TO DO

France is home to some of the greatest artists of all time. The French have produced some of the masterpieces of art, film, literature and music. It is no wonder that millions of people travel to France each year to participate in the country's cultural festivals.

Paul Cézanne (1839–1906)

A self-portrait by Paul Cézanne.

One of France's most famous painters was Paul Cézanne. Today, Cézanne is often called the father of modern painting but, in his own time, he was criticised and misunderstood. He thought the most important thing in his painting was to be able to express himself. Although it may seem strange now, this was in many ways a new concept in art. His ideas influenced other young artists who began a movement in the style of Cézanne.

Two of Cézanne's paintings are illustrated on these pages. Look carefully at the colours he used. What kind of feelings do they bring out in you? Do they make you feel warm or cold? What do you think the artist was thinking when he painted them? These are questions you can ask yourself to learn more about art.

This kind of painting is called a **still life** because none of the things in the painting can move.

Paint a portrait

Now try painting a picture yourself. Think of something or someone important in your life. It could be your teacher, your friend or a family member. It could even be you! You will need some paints, some paper and an easel. If you are doing a self-portrait, you will also need a mirror.

Further information

www.frenchentree.com/france-brittany-culture-traditions/ – introduction to Brittany's culture

www.nicecarnaval.com/htmlvers/2006/GB/frameset/frameset_1.html – the official website of the Nice Carnaval

www.saintesmaries.com/us/index.php – the website for Saintes-Maries-de-la-Mer where the Gypsy festival is held; includes pictures of the festival

www.brittany-bretagne.com/pg/culture.htm – more information and pictures about Brittany

Every effort has been made by the Publisher to ensure that these websites are suitable for children and contain no inappropriate or offensive material. However, because of the nature of the Internet, it is impossible to guarantee that the contents of these sites will not be altered. We strongly advise that Internet access is supervised by a responsible adult.

MAKE A FISH MOBILE

April Fools' Day is known as *Poisson d'Avril* in France, or 'April Fish'. It is one of the most popular festivals for children. It is a time to play tricks on people, make them believe in impossible stories and stick cut-outs of fish on their backs. In honour of the April Fish, here's a craft activity to make a fish mobile.

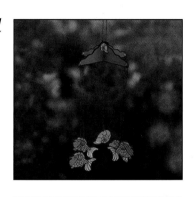

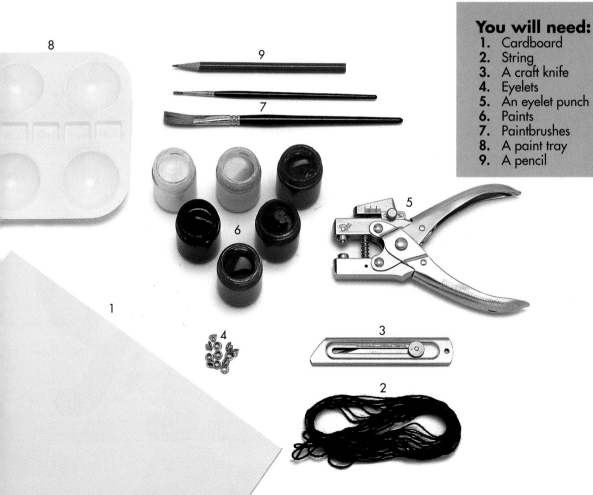

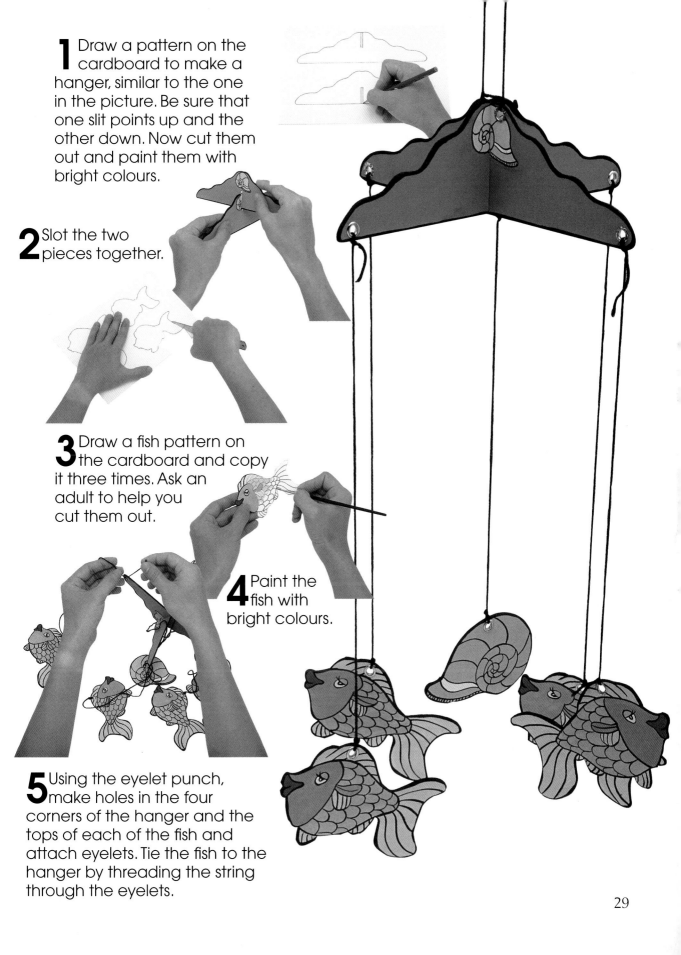

1 Draw a pattern on the cardboard to make a hanger, similar to the one in the picture. Be sure that one slit points up and the other down. Now cut them out and paint them with bright colours.

2 Slot the two pieces together.

3 Draw a fish pattern on the cardboard and copy it three times. Ask an adult to help you cut them out.

4 Paint the fish with bright colours.

5 Using the eyelet punch, make holes in the four corners of the hanger and the tops of each of the fish and attach eyelets. Tie the fish to the hanger by threading the string through the eyelets.

29

MAKE A BÛCHE DE NOËL

Bûche de Noël means 'Yule log' or 'Christmas log'. It is made with chocolate cake and ice cream and makes a delicious Christmas treat. Here's the recipe so you can make your own Christmas surprise!

You will need:

1. ½ box chocolate cake mix
2. 1 litre vanilla ice cream
3. 1 egg
4. 120 ml milk
5. Chocolate frosting
6. A mixing bowl
7. A baking tray
8. A wooden spoon
9. A butter knife
10. A spoon
11. A measuring cup
12. A chopping board
13. An oven glove

1 Mix the egg and milk with the cake mix or follow the instructions on the back of the box.

2 Pour the mixture into a baking tray. Cook according to the instructions on the box.

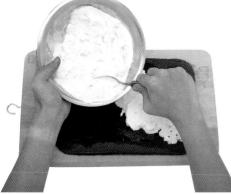

3 Let the cake cool, then spread the ice cream evenly over the cake.

4 Carefully roll the cake.

5 Ice the cake using a butter knife and decorate with holly or other Christmas decorations.

31

Glossary

apostles, 20	The twelve men Jesus Christ chose to teach Christianity.
baguettes, 4	Long, thin loaves of crusty bread.
bragon bas, 10	Baggy trousers worn by Breton men.
Celts, 4	The original settlers of France. The ancestors of the Bretons.
coiffe, 10	A tall, lace hat worn by Breton women.
crypt, 21	An underground room used as a burial place.
gadje, 21	What Gypsies call non-Gypsies.
movement, 26	A group of people who work to achieve a particular goal.
oppression, 12	To be treated unfairly or cruelly.
oratory, 20	A room or building where people go to pray.
revolution, 15	A successful attempt by a large group of people to change the political system of their country.
sabots, 10	Clogs worn by Breton men.
still life, 27	A painting or drawing of arranged objects.
tricolore, 14	The French flag.
la vendange, 24	The grape harvest.

Index